To Lachlan,
Karen's Garden

Andrew Hill

For my mother, Karen.
Her kindness, generosity,
friendship, love, and tomatoes
will never be forgotten.

Karen's Garden

By Andrew Kranichfeld
with Illustrations by Andres A. Pratts

This is the first book by author **Andrew Kranichfeld.** He hopes that *Karen's Garden* will encourage children to plant their own gardens and to see what grows. This book is also a tribute to his late mother, Karen, who was his inspiration for this story.

In 2010 Andrew lost his sight and it is also his hope that this book can be an inspiration for others to achieve their goals no matter what their circumstances or limitations.

Visit Andrew at sitebeyondsight.blogspot.com.

Andres Pratts is an illustrator living in Queens, New York. He is also a graphic designer for film and advertising.

Cover design and page layout by Libby Kingsbury

There once was a friendly, loving mother named Karen.

She had three sons, a husband, many pets,
and lots of great friends.

Of all the great things in Karen's life, her favorite place was her beautiful garden.

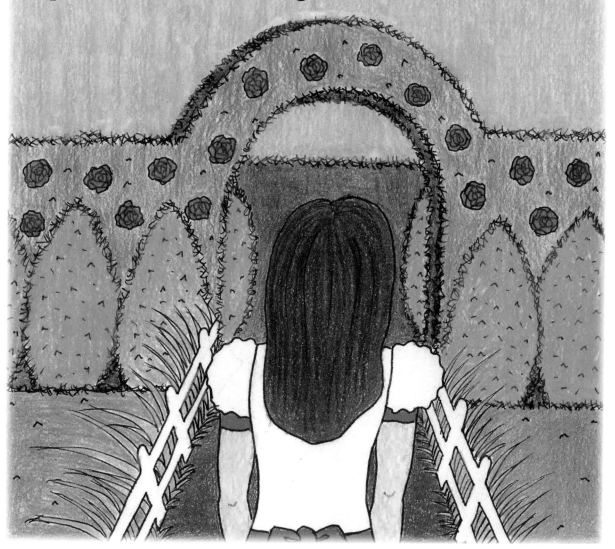

She worked in the garden every day to grow colorful flowers, fantastic fruits, and delicious vegetables.

She grew juicy watermelons and sweet corn, yellow squash and green zuchinis, large orange pumpkins and plump purple eggplants.

But of all of the things that Karen grew in her garden, she loved her tomatoes most of all.

She grew ripe red tomatoes, green tomatoes, and even bright yellow tomatoes!

She had *grape* tomatoes,

plum tomatoes,

and *cherry* tomatoes.

She was generous and would give her famous
tomatoes to many people.

She gave tomatoes to her friends, people at work, and even to the local pizza parlor!

This made the pizza man so happy that he would give her family free pizza. YUM!

Karen also loved to grow flowers in her garden.

She grew daffodils in the spring,

colorful zinnias in the summer,

and lots of beautiful roses.

Her home was always full of colorful bouquets that she made from gathering flowers from her garden.

Karen loved all of her flowers and vegetables and took very good care of them. She watered the plants every day and put plant food in the soil.

She even played music to her flowers and vegetables
because she believed it would help them grow.

But most of all Karen loved her garden
like it was part of her family.

Karen's fresh fruits, healthy vegetables,
and colorful flowers show us that
LOVE MAKES A GARDEN GROW!

Made in the USA
Charleston, SC
10 June 2016